Hot Flashes:
Maiduguri Haiku, Senryu, & Tanka

Hot Flashes

Maiduguri Haiku, Senryu, & Tanka

Richard Stevenson

Ekstasis Editions

National Library of Canada Cataloguing in Publication Data

Stevenson, Richard
  Hot flashes

  ISBN 1-896860-96-6

  I. Title.
PS8587.T479H68 2001   C811'.54   C2001-911242-4
PR9199.3.S78728H68 2001

Acknowledgements: Thanks to the editors of the following publications
in which some of these poems first appeared: *The Breath, Borders & Time,
Black Bear Review, Haiku Harvest, Haiku Moments, In Buddha's Temple,
Ku Noir, Lynx, Rags, Red Neck, Snapshots—Haiku Magazine, Stirring,
Poetry in the Light, The Poet's Cut, Stroll of Poets e-poem zine, Tanka Light,
The Worm, Zimmer Zine.*

Published in 2001 by:
Ekstasis Editions Canada Ltd.   Ekstasis Editions
Box 8474, Main Postal Outlet   Box 571
Victoria, B.C. V8W 3S1   Banff, Alberta T0L 0C0

Hot Flashes has been published with the assistance of a grant from the Canada
Council and the Cultural Services Branch of British Columbia.

Foreword

From 1980 to 1982, during the last throes of the Shehu Shagari government in Nigeria, and six months before the first of two military coups, I had the good fortune to have a two-year teaching contract with Advanced Teachers College in Maiduguri, Nigeria. I had been recruited by The World University Service of Canada and interviewed in Vancouver by a group of school superintendents from Borno State. Subsequently, I was offered the job, accepted, went to Ottawa for a week of debriefings, got all the requisite needles in the butt, and began a course of chloroquine as a prophylactic against malaria. I was required to sign a waiver that I wouldn't hold the Canadian government responsible if I came down with Lassa Fever, whatever that was (It turned out to be a nasty hemorrhagic fever with symptoms not unlike Ebola!), and I began reading everything Nigerian I could get my hands on: geographies and histories, novels, anthologies of poetry, etc.

Needless to say, nothing could prepare me for the antinomies of wealth and poverty, good will and violence, opportunity and corruption, learning and teaching I was to experience for the next two years.

I subsequently wrote and published three collections of lyric/ narrative poetry about my West African travels and experience: *Driving Offensively* (Sono Nis Press, 1985), *Horizontal Hotel: A Nigerian Odyssey* (TSAR Publications, 1989), and *Flying Coffins* (Ekstasis Editions, 1994). I thought, there: that chapter's finally finished, but no, after completing a long poem suite on the life and music of Miles Davis, *Live Evil: A Homage To Miles Davis*

(Thistledown Press, 2000), a suite which, ironically got its start from an epiphany I experienced while listening to local musicians play at a roadside shabeen in Bui, Nigeria, and turning from longer forms to haiku, senryu, and tanka about my current southern Alberta landscape and domestic life, I suddenly found the images and memories from twenty years ago flooding my consciousness. I eventually wrote enough African haiku, senryu, and tanka for a book of their own.

Doubtless, readers familiar with my other African poems will find recycled images and ideas from the earlier work here. I hope they find a good deal more concision and compression and new takes on remembered experience as well. After all, from a purely aesthetic point of view, memories and images are just more grist for the creative mill, and I was as much interested in working with the new forms as I was interested in the content while writing these brief poems.

I call them hot flashes because that is how I experienced them: as moments of red hot prickly heat and incandescence written while summer waned and fall and the first skiff of snow came on. I am middle aged now too, so the male menopause metaphor seems appropriate as well. Certainly the poems were written in tranquility, with more than a little distance and ironic bemusement behind them. I like to tell my students there may be a little snow on the roof these days, but there is still plenty of fire in the grate. I trust my memory: it hasn't gone grey the way my whiskers have, and I like the interplay between memory and desire.

Southern Alberta has been home now for fifteen years, but any nostalgia for the warmer climes of Maiduguri, Nigeria has been tempered by my memories of harsher political realities. Still, I wish to celebrate the spirit of the indominitable people I came to know as friends and neighbors there, and I hope the irony and wit that are so much a part of the senryu in English make this project worth the return mental sojourn.

I can see my breath in Lethbridge now, and, like the little engine that could, I admire the gentle plume of it and grin ruefully as I walk the family dog. The perimeter around the man-made irrigation lake is made of asphalt and shale, not laterite, and the journey pretty well ends where it began each day, instead of bifurcating into endless byways and shanties the way the roads in Maiduguri did. I take long walks for pleasure and exercise now, rather than as a means to get to work, but sometimes the interior byways throw up pithy little road signs too. Perhaps the fact that I've never owned a camera has made all the difference. Image flash bulbs seem to go off in my head all the time, like lightning flashes, momentarily throwing the entire landscape in stark relief. The senryu, with its external haiku form and satiric, sardonic human nature focus, and the tanka, with those sweet two extra lines, somehow allow me to adjust the aperture a little more than straight haiku do. *Hot Flashes* then — another blue-eyed squint through the flurry of so much western snow and flux.

waiting til it lands,
flexing forearm when it bites —
take that mosquito!

too alert to sleep,
too lazy to get the light —
you win mosquito!

starving child,
fly drinking from his eye,
doesn't blink

he thinks he's a cat!
fellow tribesmen throw real stones
when he mewls for scraps

turning the toothpick
slowly like a tinned meat key
he coils worm from flesh

when they miss the bird
sling shot stones become boulders
rolling off his roof

*juju magani** —
hands in a bowl of scorpions
Bring money, mastah!

little bush puppy
follows the sheep everywhere
and answers to *baah*

Go slow! The man cries,
broken leg bouncing in back
of commandeered van.
I no go walk again — oh!
Cop's rifle points at the stars.

*Hausa: magic medicine

twice the nicotine
in knock-off third world brands —
the filter falls off

for V.D. Chi says —
You go take am now
den go jiggy jig

One Great Hitler Photo Studio
the hand-painted sign screams.
Click. Click. Click.

Moji's Hair Saloon —
style silhouettes on a board
on a tree

burrs in rasta hair
cola nut crumb on spittle
rises, falls, rises and falls

Geisha, other brands —
same mackerel leaps over
perfect tomato

If constipated
order the Cornish pasties
the vet expat says

Prayer Is Telephone To God
the bumper snicker says —
prayer mat on the dash

on the cab window
silhouette of Africa
upside down

Ramadan —
students jump from their desks
spit out the windows

concertina-ribbed
boy marches in the helmet
of his begging bowl

*Twenty kobo, sah
I go be miguardi* now.*
Can't escape my car.

*corruption of English: My guard.

Cabbie wants
twenty naira dash or no go
open luggage boot

under the beaming
buckwheat billboard sign
kwashiokor kid!

Sallah —
goat bleats
from the cab trunk!

Tender lion steak?
Sah? Is beef —
e come from de cow

Horizontal Hotel —
whore house
or morgue?

nineteenth robbery —
I move in with a friend
and get robbed again!

not golf clubs for sale
but vulture heads-and-necks
beaked to the bowl

Daheru's business
selling water from my taps.
Villagers line up
with yokes and rusty buckets
from huts across the tracks.

road kill is it?
something indeterminate
in a white singlet*

*British: undershirt

to avoid beatings
hold-up candidates carry
wads of single notes

in a go-slow
thieves work the cars on foot,
pass collection plates

In Lagos the thieves
are so slick and organized
they book appointments!

When the hotel clerk
learns I'm off to Lagos next
he refunds my bill

I drop my wallet
in a busy market place —
a vendor hands it back

outside Leventis
artificial Christmas trees,
three lepers with bowls

harmattan —
the old crooner himself
sings "White Christmas."

among paper wads
piles of human excrement,
giant scrotum pods!

Christmas in Kano —
Van, our black Santa Claus
in red piped pyjamas

harmattan —
even our coffee table
covered in sand

Nguru* stampede!
Cattle sort themselves as cars,
turn into driveways!

Nguru kung fu —
a man squats before the screen,
pisses in the sand

*town near Nigeria/Niger border

new bature's house —
plaster and shit
in the bathtub

swish, swish, flush —
Sale holds the shirt collar
for the rinse cycle

new staff quarters:
three bedrooms, tub, toilet,
shower with no drain

in the bath tub
on a paisley island shirt
chameleon grins

African potlatch?
As King Sunny Ade plays
and women shimmy,
men slide bills down their foreheads;
women tuck them in brassieres.

for you, customer:
he pours potatoes quickly,
hides the false bottom

hoopoes' flight pattern
up and down as he flap rests
flaps in Sahel heat

never a straight path,
Abyssinian Roller
cavorts with thermals

Peugot 504 —
not just a middle class car
but an hula* too!

*hula, Hausa n., cylindrical hat decorated in distinctive bar pat-
tern embroidery: named for significant persons, things, events,
etc.

sweeping, sweeping
to get to hard pan beneath
the Muslim faithful

On their prayer mats
chanting Koranic verses
under tall green neems
novices at their devotions —
wasp bottoms pulse on fruit rinds.

little agama
what are you thinking when you
cock your head at me?

pin-striped alhaji
slipping into a neem's shade?
no, a blue-tailed skink.

fresh-picked cotton bolls?
no, just toilet paper wads
among the milkweeds

resting his shovel,
the gardener drops his pants
and shits on the lawn

Pepé or pankay —
savoury or sweet dough balls
deep-fried while you wait.
How could Tim Horton's staff find
the love in this woman's hands?

imagine Shiva
held pom poms in all her hands —
my heart jumps, thorn tree

agamas in hcat
faster than toy road race cars,
your hormones pile up

both buckets full —
muscles bigger than most men's,
her black brassiere spills

shoe backs tacked down
to make clogs of his slip-ons,
his round heels shine.

Doing a post-Doc
on keloid scars and tattoos,
her learning's under wraps.

Banner headline screams
"Five Hundred dead in Kano" —
next day, three fifty

Trudeau arrives —
Canadian flag is raised
upside down

Trudeau lays a wreath —
photo on the front page
shows his ass

party for Trudeau —
state governor's bodyguards
carry empty guns

fearsome Tuareg guard
face covered but for his eyes'
smile crinkles

Everyone asleep —
the guard pissed when I arrive,
see his girlfriend's breasts.
I wish to leave a package;
he reaches for an arrow.

shit alley —
pass squatters as easily
as a well-formed stool

"…piles of shit for sale!"
bature appalled at what
turn out to be eels

traffic sign
on the Bama road
says "Go!"

slow to sixty —
then skull and cross bones, the words,
"You were warned!"

airline logo
an elephant with wings —
we just clear the tarmac

add water and stir —
Nido powdered milk
gives you dysentery

no weight restrictions?
asphalt like runelled snow —
a record that skips

strange light in the sky —
a semi with one wonky eye
looks to the desert

another semi —
inside back tire the wrong size
doesn't touch pavement

turn the corner —
the highway disappears!
no earthquake, just rain

scarabs push shit balls —
my V.W. bug pushes
sun over the hill

cumbersome beetle
clanks along in bright armour
cries like a baby

their "pink teacher" —
how her gold arm hairs glisten!
wheat in winter sun

sun a blood orange
in harmattan haze —
can almost taste it

smouldering trash heap —
for the children of Gwonge
big rock candy hill

"You Canadians!
you always want things done right!"
the Hausa clerk says

"*Ina zua*,"*
the clerk says, stamping my file,
walking out the back

They forgot the drain…
Karl sweeps the shower water
out a low wall pipe,
deftly replaces the steel wool
used to keep the roaches out

*Hausa: I'm coming

petrol shortage —
pump jockey sucks a litre
from a wreck out back.
"Don't want you to think bad things
about my country," he says.

same gulping movement:
gas hose disgorging petrol,
snake swallowing prey

Same sentence for rape
as for smoking gange at school,
the principal says.
The victims are only girls,
their place is working at home.

broken bottle shards
embedded in the fence cap —
not a winsome grin

awakened by thieves —
fridge now a monolith
in the desert sand

big man by her bed!
in daylight by barred windows
a child's rubber thongs

Well, they weren't Igbo
Chi says, looking at the mess.
You still have your fans.

not even Christmas —
still, Bing's golden tonsils
assail desert air

There! Can you see?
Worms swim toward light shining
in the patient's eye

seen from a distance
cattle at a water hole —
not flies, open sores

mosquito larvae
and whirligig beetles swim
in the hotel pool

in Nguru
Bruce Lee on the screen —
locals jump kick stars

Quixotic lizards
bob heads when I get too close.
Wise elder statesmen.

Talk about stoners!
The villagers sell pot in
cement bag croissants.

Small epiphany:
oranges aren't orange, but green;
are sour here, not sweet

two cups of coffee —
my hands begin to tremble.
African instant!

twice the tar,
three times the nicotine…
the filter falls off!

Chi has good news!
Cops busted a den of thieves,
"tortured them proper."

by my bedside:
pipe, knife, box of matches,
jar of gasoline

petrol shortage —
pump at a rakish angle,
fumes and cigarettes

new secretary,
fingers one off the home keys —
the principal's niece

shades of Graham Greene:
greenhouse smell of fecund earth,
weight of hot, moist air

"Don't spit," the signs say —
not that I'd considered it
in the airport hall.
Then the fast of Ramadan;
my students will not swallow.

Quel kuti? I ask.
How much for crocodile teeth?
(A gift for my friend
who sculpts in rare ivories)
Kai! I must buy the whole head?!

some pharmacy this —
animal skulls arranged
in descending size!

Manga, Nguru —
mud huts, guinea corn fences…
English mints for sale!

to get his picture
you must pretend to shoot me —
or pay through the nose!

not stealing their souls
but taking a shed skin, see —
the money to eat!

This chameleon —
Adam's Family toy bank's
detached wind-up hand
makes a quick grab for the coin
and the hand that feeds it

Easy Bake ovens —
cinder block, tin-roofed houses
of bature fools.

Forgive me, madam.
I didn't think my ice cubes
would scare you so much.
I wished to cool the water,
not make eyes big as the fridge.

Bolori layout —
shanty town across the tracks
a mouth of bad teeth

the woman smiles,
teeth blood red from cola nut —
whose hen house then?

"Bring money," they say,
meaning we've settled on
the white price

prayer mat on the dash,
his rosary hangs from
the rear view mirror

Caffenol decals,
Maggi, girls in bikinis —
any logo's fine,
even Rorschach Africa
on back window upside down.

In heavy traffic
steady tattoo on the horn,
brakes that really chirp!
And to think we used to take
our canaries into caves…

vultures hang around —
glum reporters in great coats
and wet fedoras

post-independence —
hotel pool offers cool leaves
and insect larvae

staying in Lagos —
hotel clerk proffers room key
and bathtub plug

Lagos go-slow:
thieves take up a collection
window by window

gorgeous dinner guest
rises from the next table —
"make I go shit now."

sign in a disco:
No Dancing Alone
No Bathroom Slippers

"We only rent rooms
to ladies," the desk clerk says.
Wives don't qualify.

not pop, minerals —
as in mineral water,
more chic than sugar

almost transparent —
little geckos behind
our white toilet tank

wide wale tribal scars
in distinctive stripes —
their cat-clawed faces smile

Peace is from the south,
cross carved into her forehead —
Igbo Christian brand

Akwai Coke? I ask.
She draws up the cool bottle
radium fuel rod

Ah! Cool kiosk Coke.
"Ba changey." The urchin's eyes
feint from Nido tin.

Highway 61!
Dylan among home made
highlife and Hausa tapes

In Maiduguri
you can't buy a case of beer
without the empties!
How to score an empty case:
the zen koan for thirsty minds.

single rubber thong —
paramecium-shaped sign
on the refuse heap

Mercedes —
blue-tailed skink
amidst agamas

mud hut with a straw roof —
inside on colour T.V.
Charlie's Angels dance!

Lake Chad Club —
gecko runs down the valance
across the T.V.

In the outdoor bar
we watch agamas in heat —
a child's road race set

Queued for the signal,
we dash to get to the plane.
Elderly women
ignore the falling clatter —
enamel and calabash.

Sannu bature,
Abi you want jiggy jig?
Girl gyrates hips

Nice play, Shakespeare —
"Dem go ask for jiggy jig
no go get jiggy jig."

Dash me ten kobo!
the market urchin demands.
A bite in the apple

outside Leventis —
three lepers with begging bowls.
fake Christmas trees fall.

in the freezer case
the frozen turkeys salaam
faceless facing east

Yankari Reserve —
I wake to warthog snorting
five feet from my head

lion country —
four batures draw straws for
who will change the tire

outside Cotonou —
young man with iguana ducks
the Kodak moment

"How much for the pair?"
Male and female python skins —
his and hers towels

Abomey gift shop —
the letter openers
miniature swords

Abomey giftshop —
serviette rings the shape of
Dahomean thrones

amazed they still stand —
walls of the Fon king's compound
mud and human blood

Abomey, Benin —
Guernica-like appliqué
table cloths for sale
at the museum's exit.
Beheaded silhouette men.

the Fon king's throne
carved iron wood perched atop
four Portuguese skulls

wasps' bottoms throb
on smashed gash of rotten fruit —
the Muslim boys pray

weaver bird holds
the shiny full moon
above satchel purse

the cabbie's at fault:
cops leave him slumped in his seat
where he bleeds to death

Wrong place and wrong time:
kids wail on my car with sticks
in Islamic zeal.
Ridding the 'hood of harlots —
my car a grub among ants.

"Feed well, grow strong" —
billboard macaroni shot
of a smiling boy.
Pot-bellied kid marches by,
his begging bowl his helmet.

"Dogs aren't kept as pets,"
Zavin explains as he veers
toward the skittish pup

no water, no food —
the skittish bush dog sits chained
to an old car wreck

What are you in for?
the thawed, re-frozen turkeys
seem to ask the fish

Once stricken, twice shy —
the Maiduguri two-step
makes Karl improvise:
eat nothing that isn't canned,
store cutlery in the fridge.

You go buy am beef?
The meat man swats flies off
his very best piece

Ponded yam? I ask,
not thinking of misspellings —
Nicer without *u*

'snot soup — or is it?!
My spoon draws the glutinous
post-nasal okra

Looking for eyeballs,
slowly, carefully, I spoon
up my goat's head soup

Opening the fridge,
Karl sits with cool cutlery
in a halo of white light

Folks in Potiskum
pronounce the *p* as an *f*.
Phigger that one out!

a spiked two-by-four,
four cement-filled oil drums:
effective road block.

raw, open sewers —
two scarabs push, somersault
over one dung ball

oranges are green!
sour, fibrous, full of seeds —
sucked, squeezed, not eaten.

They don't flash the bird,
but open fists twice, palms out:
fifth son of fifth wife!

Magic egg sandwich —
could be egg salad, hard-boiled
come quick quick
or when you return for beer
two hours after you gave up!

overweight women
are desired, much prized here:
well-fed means well-healed

Cabbie is confused,
wants us to raise his child,
not just babysit.
Na we have money plenty?
Na dis be good for Bintu?

The Wabenzi tribe?
Dem who drive Mercedes,
have naira plenty.

Villagers don't just
balance those bowls on their heads —
they use woven rings!
And to think our models learn
to strut their stuff with fat books…

African cook book —
not cups of this or that
but tobacco tins!

King Sunny Ade —
well-healed dancer dashes*
the on-stage roadie
for a great guitar solo,
peels wad to rising drumbeats.

juju concert —
dancer dashes guitarist
to a rising beat

*African slang: bribes.

Remember phosphates?
Still in the detergents here
but *our* hands are clean

outdoor juju
sofas around the tennis court
for rich *alhajis*

Target brand —
twice the tar and nicotine
of western brands

clitorectomies —
so our women will not stray…
I think: we spay pets

flying home —
looking down on the clouds,
I see tastebuds